TABLE OF CONTENTS

- Leveraging Operational Intelligence -
The Battle of Tannenberg and Masurian Lakes (1914)

"Know the enemy, know yourself; your victory will never be endangered." -Sun Tzu-[1]

Leveraging operational intelligence remains the cornerstone for managing uncertainty, fog, and friction of war in this era of seemingly endless advances in battlefield awareness and information dominance. The study of strategy, tactics, and operational art, teaches that information about the battlespace is essential for successful warfare.[2] Not only information about enemy, but information about yourself as well. The distillate of enemy information is intelligence. Information assurance denotes acquiring intelligence, regardless of source. Conversely, information denial includes all efforts to protect one's own intelligence from the enemy.

The challenge for the intelligence practitioner is not new. Indeed, examples from the past provide relevant insights into how contemporary military commanders resemble their counterparts from nearly a century ago. The Battle of Tannenberg and Masurian Lakes, Russia's 1914 push to invade Eastern Prussia, was a disastrous defeat for Moscow due in large part to German exploitation of Signals, Human, and Imagery intelligence. Strategic decisions exploiting these three disciplines dramatically altered the course of this engagement. Rapid implementation of operational intelligence by the German commanders hastened their victory. Russian indifference to their own warfare vulnerabilities led to catastrophic losses.

Intelligence Paradigms

Perhaps unexpectedly, operational intelligence experiences from WWI are germane today and for the future. Uncertainty and confusion have always predominated war. Carl von Clausewitz describes the uncertainty of war, *"In war more than anywhere else, things do not turn out as we expect."*[3] However, even the expectations of a military genius must be based on a minimum of intelligence if one is to implement the principles of war.[4] The Battle of Tannenberg and Masurian Lakes illustrates the German ability to leverage operational intelligence so that their expectations were more predictive and uncertainty diminished.

Is it possible to know too much about an enemy's situation? Might operational decisions be delayed or hindered while a commander waits for the latest intelligence, anticipating the possibility of shifting forces as a result? Today, that risk is mitigated by all source fusion and assimilated displays. But at the beginning of the twentieth century, a modern field army, with its artillery and long supply trains, did not have the ability to respond quickly to either challenges or opportunities. The risk of issuing orders and counter-orders, resulting in disorder was very real. Therefore, as intelligence technology improved, there developed a variance between what a commander learned and one's ability to influence a timely response. A technological inconsistency underscored the gap between speedy communications and primitive mobility. Rapid incorporation of intelligence therefore was a formidable task, mastered only by superb armies. Even though timely intelligence gave a commander more options, WWI maneuver was still determined by the muscles of men and horses.[5]

Traditional theories regarding operational intelligence will form the framework for examining decisions made by the German commanders during the Battle of Tannenberg. Moreover, Russian failure to appreciate the value of operational intelligence will be shown to have doomed their campaign.

Setting the Stage

The year 1914 found Europe in a state of armed suspense. Two great political and military alliances stood facing each other. France and Russia, which had formed an alliance in 1892 against the perceived hegemony of a strengthening Germany, had seen their fears come to fruition. Germany, Austria-Hungry and Italy were prepared for a great war ranging across the continent.

France and Russia developed a plan to fight the German alliance on two fronts. A key aspect of their plan was to force the Alliance into dispersing its forces east and west thus preventing it from establishing a preponderance of strength in either theater. France and Russia planned to crush the enemy with superior manpower along both fronts. The plan called for a Russian advance to draw a large German force toward the eastern front so the French offensive would have a greater chance of success, seeking to optimize its operational advantages.

Strengths of Opposing Forces

The Battle of Tannenberg and Masurian Lakes pitted the Russian First and Second Armies against the German Eighth Army. The First Army consisted of 86 battalions of infantry and 120 cavalry squadrons. The Second Army was comprised of

164 battalions of infantry and 110 cavalry squadrons. Total Russian soldiers were estimated at 500,000. In contrast, 144 battalions of infantry and 84 cavalry squadrons comprised the German Eighth Army. Whereas the German soldiers numbered less than half those of the Russians, they enjoyed a superior ten to one ratio of heavy artillery. Additionally, the Germans had better-quality vehicles, food, communications equipment, medical and logistic infrastructure, as well as professional training. [6]

The Commanders

On the day following the declaration of war by Germany, August 2, 1914, the Russian Czar appointed his uncle, the Grand Duke Nikolai Nikolaievich Romanov, as Supreme Commander in Chief. Nikolai was an accomplished soldier with extensive experience in cavalry commands. General Yakov Zilinsky, 60 years old, was Commander of the Russian Northwest Front. He was more of a staff officer than a commander in the field. Zilinsky's responsibility included the First Army commanded by General Pavel Rennenkampf, and the Second Army commanded by General Alexander Samsonov. Both men were in their 60's, in poor health, and considered questionable leaders, although respected for their courage. Rennenkampf had seen battle against the Chinese and Japanese. His relationship with his staff was fractious. Samsonov had experienced combat but had been in semi-military retirement since 1909 as Governor of Turkestan. He was popular with his troops and approachable. Opinion in the Russian Army was divided as to whether he or Rennenkampf was the better commander.

The Chief of the German General Staff was Colonel General Helmuth von Moltke. In command of the Eighth Army was Colonel General Max von Prittwitz.

Prittwitz was 66 when the war began having served in the Army for 49 years. He had won the Iron Cross and was considered a fine officer. His Chief of Staff was Brigadier General Georg von Waldersee. Colonel Max Hoffmann, a Russian military expert and a strong proponent of operational intelligence, was the Eighth Army Operations Officer.[7] During the course of the Tannenberg battle, Moltke relieved Prittwitz and Waldersee, replacing them with General Paul von Hindenburg and Major General Erich Ludendorff respectively. Hindenburg, at age 67, was already a hero of Germany and an army icon. Ludendorff was 49 at the beginning of the war. He was a keen tactician with experience on the German General Staff.[8] The foresight of these commanders to employ intelligence collection methods and to use battlefield intelligence in operations, was the crucial factor in turning back the Russian advance.

The Battle of Tannenberg and Masurian Lakes

The Battle of Tannenberg and Masurian Lakes was actually a series of fierce engagements between Russian and German forces from August 17th through 30th, 1914. Following the Franco-Russian plan, France attacked Germany from the west. Russian forces took to the field before their mobilization was complete in order to exert pressure on Germany and draw forces away from France. As anticipated by the Germans, the Russian First and Second Armies headed rapidly for eastern Prussia, but their rear echelon support services were much slower to organize. Leading elements of the armies would never see many necessary items such as field bakeries and ambulance wagons. Moreover, shortages of telephone wire and telegraph equipment, as well as trained signal corps troops, would make quick, dependable communications impossible.[9]

For expediency, the Russians had planned to use existing telegraph lines in captured German territory; however, they ultimately discovered local communications systems destroyed by retreating forces. Consequently, the Russians resorted to sending messages by wireless radio - but not in code because their divisional staffs lacked cryptographers. To the Russians, the risks of using codes which the recipient might not decipher, seemed more of a danger than German monitoring of every possible frequency.[10] Moreover, poorly trained telegraphers were unable to send simple messages without confusion, let alone coded ones. Thus, wireless messages in the clear became a standard Russian practice, to the delight of permanent listening stations of the Espionage and Counterintelligence Department of the German General Staff at Thorn, Posen and Konigsberg, which tracked Russian radio traffic.[11]

As the two Russian armies advanced into eastern Prussia, they had to make their way around a series of marshes and wetlands known as the "Masurian Lakes." Tactical plans called for the First Army to swing north around the Masurian Lakes from the east, forcing the German Eighth Army's retreat toward the Second Army which was approaching from the south side of the Lakes. The Russians planned to envelop the Germans and destroy them before they could fall back to Konigsberg. This plan relied heavily on close coordination between the two Russian commanders and wireless radio was their primary means of contact.

The first suspected use of intelligence deception during Tannenberg turned out to be false. Since 1910, the Konigsberg intelligence office believed Russian doctrine called for massive cavalry raids into East Prussia using their vast numbers of horseman. In actual practice, the Russian cavalry confined itself to patrol and intelligence sorties.

The difference between expectation and reality gave the Germans reason to wonder if they had been deliberately fed false information. Infact, German analysis had been incorrect.[12]

On the other hand, the Germans intimately understood the geography of eastern Prussia with its maze of wetlands and quagmires. They knew, the Russians could only advance by sending one army north and the other south around the Masurian Lakes. Prittwitz calculated that by concentrating Eighth Army forces successively against each Russian army, he could martial superior forces to defeat each army in turn. This is an excellent example of intelligence being used to leverage operational art factors of distance and force deployment.

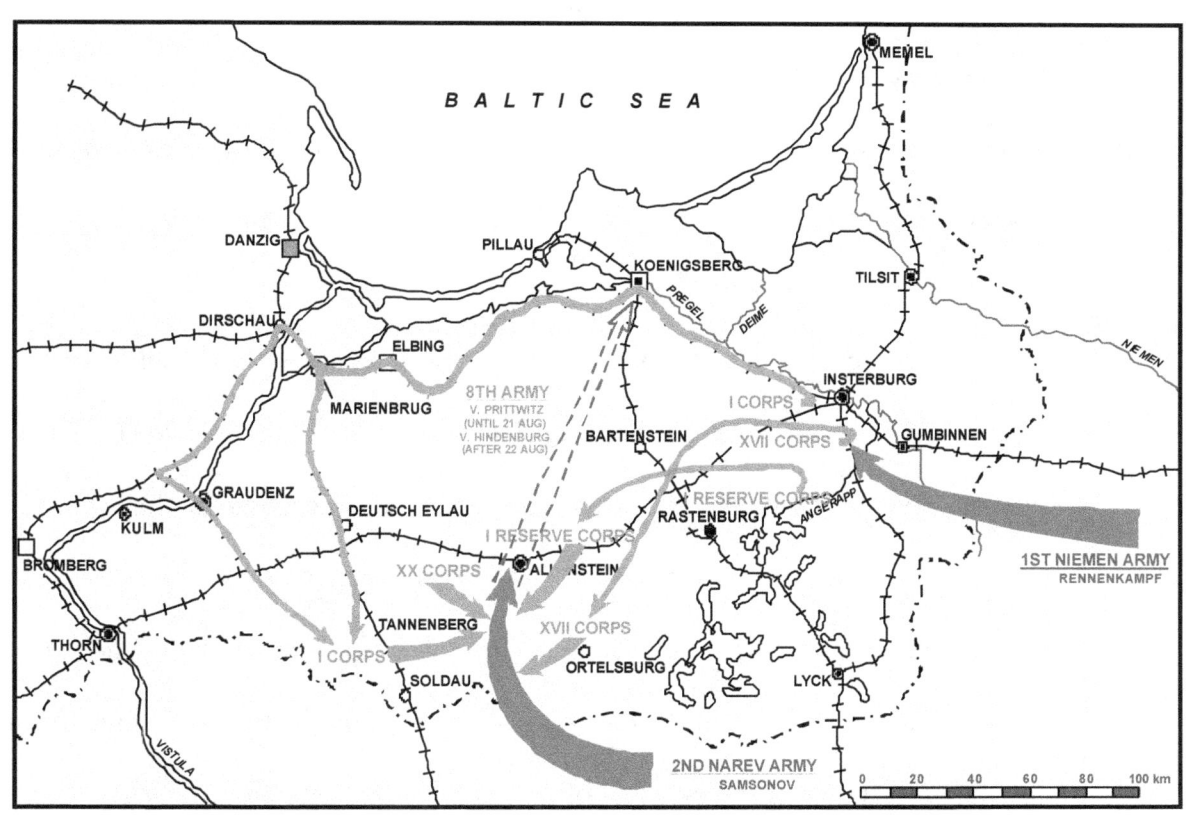

Colonel Hoffmann, Prittwitz's Operations Officer, had studied the two Russian generals and knew Rennenkampf and Samsonov each carried a measure of personal enmity for the other. Hoffmann, as an intelligence advocate, closely followed the biographies of his opponents and predicted the two Russian Generals would have trouble coordinating.[13] He was right.

Rennenkampf's First Army began moving on August 13th, four days ahead of the Second Army. The Germans knew immediately. One key source of intelligence for the German Eighth Army consisted of reconnaissance reports from airplanes, new to the battlefield landscape. German pilots reported sightings of long columns of Rennenkampf's supply wagons and brigade elements moving toward the North. At the same time, they reported seeing nothing to the South. Hoffmann recalled, *"...as the airmen's reports still continued to show that no movement of troops could be observed on the roads coming from the south, (Prittwitz) decided to prepare the mass of the army for the attack on the (First) Army."*[14]

Prittwitz kept his options open, incorporating operational intelligence, in this case from aerial observations. He used this intelligence to reassess his defense plan. Pilot reports had given Prittwitz the information he needed to concentrate his forces against the First Army, knowing the Russian Second was too far away and moving too slowly to be a factor - another example where the Germans leveraged operational intelligence to capitalize on foreknowledge of the enemy.[15] Consequently, by the time Rennenkampf's troops entered Prussian territory, most of the Eighth Army was poised to strike.

As the Russian First Army crossed into eastern Prussia, they observed boys, mostly ages twelve to fifteen, on bicycles hurrying away from the approaching columns.

As it turned out, this was part of an efficient human intelligence system organized by the Germans. Using clandestine agents to report on the situation, the Germans employed young people on bicycles to hover around the columns. Sometimes they used soldiers disguised as peasants or women, or placed people in the high fire-watch towers in forested area as observation posts.[16] This proved an invaluable source of operational intelligence for Prittwitz. On the other hand, Rennenkampf failed to take appropriate security measures. As his forces seized German territory, they were susceptible to observation from a hostile local populace.

From August 17th through the 20th, the two armies clashed with mixed success. Casualties and losses mounted on both sides. The Germans were driven back at Gumbinnen and Prittwitz became increasingly concerned when his pilots began sighting vanguards of Samsonov's Second Army south of the Masurian Lakes. On the 20th, a document was found on a dead Russian officer that contained details of the Russian plan.[17] At the same time, German headquarters intercepted a radiogram that referred to the overall offensive, and contained an attack order confirming what the Germans had deduced from the document found on the dead Russian officer. The Second Army was to meet with the First in a pincer movement overwhelming the Germans. Signals intelligence thus confirmed earlier German document exploitation.

On the evening of the 20th, Rennenkampf sent a halt order to his commanders by wireless in a simple code. A German mathematics professor, working as a cryptographer for the Eighth Army, deciphered the message with no difficulty. Based on the intercepted halt order and the knowledge that the First Army would remain in place, the Germans decided quietly to pull back and head south to engage the arriving Second

Army. Rennenkampf, unaware that the German withdrawal was due to intelligence collection and analysis, wrongly believed his forces had overwhelmed the German defenses.

Rennenkampf's own reconnaissance capability, based primarily on mounted cavalry, failed miserably to report on the German positions. Rather than scouting behind enemy forces, cavalry regularly dismounted when fired upon although there were opportunities for avoiding danger by bold horsemanship. The Russian cavalry might have determined much more about German forces and provided valuable troop locations were it not for overly cautious doctrine and practice.[18] Furthermore, the First Army was in no shape to pursue the Germans. Rather, it used this halt period to reconstitute. Rennenkampf did not know that the Germans were intercepting his situational messages back to General Zilinsky. Meanwhile, communication from Zilinsky's headquarters was often cause for complaint because it arrived in garbled form. This could only have been due to inefficient operators at the receiving end, for the Germans had no difficulty understanding them.[19]

To the German High Command, Eighth Army's retirement toward the south seemed like a failure of nerve. Prittwitz never made it clear to Berlin that his use of operational intelligence, gleaned from radio intercepts, was largely responsible for his maneuvering of forces. Perhaps it was fear of compromising the source, or desire to appear tactically brilliant, but Prittwitz did not reveal the radio intercepts. The German High Command replaced Prittwitz and Waldersee, despite their having developed a winning strategy against the invading Russians.[20]

Nevertheless, Moltke gave the Eighth Army to General Paul von Hindenburg and Major General Erich Ludendorff became Chief of Staff. Hoffmann remained as Operations Officer. When Hindenburg and Ludendorff learned of the radio intercepts from Hoffmann, they acceded to quietly rely on the same source of operational intelligence for tactical decisions. Prittwitz had already masterfully leveraged operational intelligence.[21]

With new commanders, the German Eighth Army continuously monitored Russian movements via air reconnaissance and radio intercepts. It eventually took up positions near Tannenberg, ahead of the arriving Second Army. Given foreknowledge of the exact route the Russians would take around the Masurian Lakes, the Germans leveraged operational intelligence and utilized terrain to their advantage. As it turned out, Samsonov's army had overextended their operational reach. Soldiers had been struggling through the marshy terrain for days without adequate food or rest. Troops were exhausted and expended, in no condition for battle, and unaware of the German trap. Realizing their advantage, the Germans confidently shifted to engage Samsonov and maximize the element of surprise.

Rennenkampf's First Army, receiving practically no intelligence from its cavalry, continued its cautious advance toward Konigsberg convinced they had routed the Germans. In truth, the Germans were by no means in disorder, and the optimistic reports which reached Rennenkampf emanated from friendly Polish inhabitants. No effort was made to verify these reports, which were passed on as facts to General Zilinsky."[22]

Not all collected intelligence emboldened the Germans. An aerial report, coupled with a radio intercept, indicated an intensely strong Russian First Army element, poised to thrust through Angerburg and overwhelm the German forces. However, by clever maneuver, the Germans neutralized the Russian advantage in yet another example of leveraging operational intelligence.[23]

On August 25th, Rennenkampf transmitted a complete operations order to the First Army's IV Corps. Half an hour later, Samsonov sent a priority message to his XIII Corps pertaining to operations for the day. Both messages were sent in plain text and the Konigsberg listening station rejoiced. For the Germans, this was an intelligence windfall. Rennenkampf was clearly not a threat and both armies were unaware of the impending danger. Furthermore, the two Russian armies were tending to move away from each other rather than uniting their forces. A thorough intelligence analysis convinced the Germans they could prosecute Samsonov's isolated army for at least four or five days before assistance could arrive. Capitalizing on this opportunity, Hindenburg diverted all of his Eighth Army resources from their westward withdrawal to attack Samsonov's army, which was now approaching the vicinity of Tannenberg.[24]

Still unaware of the Germans to his front, Samsonov was also planning an aggressive movement, despite his commanders' call for a halt and resupply. Zilinsky had been insistent that the Second Army engage the Germans at the earliest opportunity and was enraged that Samsonov had yet to see the enemy. Samsonov was determined to press ahead without a break, regardless of his troops' condition. Communications between Samsonov and Zilinsky (all intercepted) show an alarming awareness of his own intelligence shortfalls and of his enemy's strengths, yet Samsonov forged ahead. *"The frontier roads are very heavy. Reconnaissances [sic] therefore were only short. Enemy aeroplanes followed the movements of the Army all the time,"* Samsonov reported.[25] He clearly knew his own intelligence was lacking and German aerial observation of his troop movements made him vulnerable. Furthermore, telegraph wire was in short supply and working lines were often cut by saboteurs or unfriendly locals. Second Army was so widely dispersed, that dispatch riders were of little use. Faced with these problems, Samsonov used uncoded wireless radio for communication, choosing between two evils: interception on one hand, incomprehensibility on the other.[26] Interception of Second Army radio traffic gave the Germans further assurance that the Russian opposition would be severely diminished. This leveraging of operational intelligence directly enabled the Germans to seize the initiative.[27]

On August 26th, the Germans attacked the Second Army's positions across a number of fronts, overwhelming the Russian artillery and using infantry in a series of quick rushes that drove back the Russian forces. By nightfall, the battered Russians were retreating southward, away from any possible assistance from Rennenkampf's First Army. During this time, the Germans intercepted a Russian radiogram revealing that Rennenkampf had been finally directed to proceed south to aid Samsonov. In response, the German 1st Cavalry Division was ordered to halt the advance of the Rennenkampf's lead elements. From the morning of the 27th until the 29th, the Germans remained one step ahead of the Russian movements through the interception of signals, the analysis of the Russian plans, and the redirection of Eighth Army assets to counter the Russian objectives; a masterful integration of operational intelligence.

Indicative of Russian intelligence failures, Zilinsky had only a sporadic and fragmentary understanding of the situation facing his two armies. Rennenkampf was being ordered to advance on Konigsberg while at the same time, sending reinforcements south to assist Samsonov. The Germans were ahead of every movement with defenses prepared. They slowed Rennenkampf's progress on all fronts. Rennenkampf's cavalry was still not giving him any ground intelligence. He was effectively stumbling in the blind.

On the 29th and 30th, the Germans intercepted a number of radio messages that mentioned Rennenkampf's frustration and inability to make progress. The last radiogram made it clear that Rennenkampf had no further intention of advancing to the west or southwest, making it possible for the Eighth Army to focus on the remnants of Samsonov's army.[28]

Between August 29th and 30th, the Germans chased, tormented, and massacred Second Army soldiers as shattered elements tried, amid growing panic, to escape through the marshes, swamps and forests around the Masurian Lakes.[29] All the while, the Germans were following the defeat through frantic Russian radio messages. One Russian survivor said, *"Whenever our units took the offensive, the Germans, without meeting the challenge, would roll their line back, and bring our attacking units under their machine-gun fire."*[30] Using signals intelligence, the Germans successfully isolated the Second Army leaving them with little chance of escape.

On August 31st, Zilinsky finally judged the battle to be lost and ordered all remaining Second Army units to retire eastward, leaving the units inside the German cordon to their fate. Samsonov, in utter despair for his leadership failure, committed suicide in the woods of Masurian Lakes while his staff disintegrated.[31]

After destroying the Second Army, the Germans focused full attention on Rennenkampf's First Army, still occupying territory east of Konigsberg. Captured papers at Tannenberg gave the Germans a good sense of First Army's force disposition. Additionally, aircraft observation continued to aid German operational intelligence.[32] Hindenburg, exploiting Rennenkampf's lack of communication security, dealt the Russians blow after blow. By September 10th, Rennenkampf had been forced to retreat though he kept his withdrawal orderly enough to avoid the disaster suffered by Samsonov's Second Army.[33]

Accounts of casualties vary widely owing to the enormity of the figures. First Army losses during the invasion of East Prussia were calculated to be 30,000 killed; 70,000 taken prisoner; and 622 guns captured.[34] Second Army losses were 75,000 killed; 92,000 taken prisoner; and 300 guns captured.[35] Another historical study places total Russian losses at 310,000.[36] In addition to the loss of prestige, the Russians lost a vast amount of materiel, which would not be replaced at any time during World War I.

Reflections

The Battle of Tannenberg and Masurian Lakes was the greatest defeat suffered by any of the belligerents during the war and had enormous political ramifications.[37] It stands as a case study of numerous errors and contributing misjudgments on the part of the Russians and became a tragic and unnecessary testament to Russia's unpreparedness in leadership and materiel.

Leveraging operational intelligence is a function of three elements. First, the intelligence professional must ensure the key data is available, not just massive data of all sorts. The German intelligence system forwarded only key data to their field commanders. In the contemporary intelligence collection environment, technological advances have created a parallel increase in the shear volume of intelligence. Key data is sometimes harder to identify.

Secondly, the data collected must be correctly analyzed. German analysis had mixed success, just like present-day efforts. The predicted employment of Russian cavalry was wrong, but animosity between the Russian commanders was correctly deduced. German analysis determined the worth of intelligence.

Finally, sound operational intelligence, that which is "actionable," must be highlighted for the decision-maker.[38] Commanders must put aside any preconceived notions about the nature of operational intelligence. A bias toward skepticism or over confidence concerning the usefulness of operational intelligence, will distort the decision making process. Consequently, key data, properly analyzed and given context, must be presented to the commander in such a way that its utility is self-evident. Leveraging operational intelligence, therefore, enables a commander to reduce the uncertainty, fog, and friction of war.[39]

Baron Antoine-Henri de Jomini provided detailed insights on operational intelligence which reflected Napoleon's own appreciation for its utility and value.[40] Intelligence activities which Jomini believed were the most reliable are remarkably relevant for present-day commanders: 1) A highly organized and efficient system of human espionage; 2) Reconnaissance by special units; 3) The interrogation of prisoners of war; 4) Systematic analysis of courses of action open to the enemy; and 4) Signals.[41] One can conclude that the Germans emphasized all five aspects. In doing so, the Germans were able to attain information superiority at Tannenberg.

In modern lexicon, information superiority is the capability to collect, process, and disseminate an uninterrupted flow of information while exploiting or denying an adversary's ability to do the same. Information superiority increases the speed at which decisions are made, while preempting enemy choices and courses of action.[42] An amazing aspect of Tannenberg was the German achievement of information superiority using both high and low-technology methods, as defined by the period, while the Russians failed to do the same.

Sometimes the biggest problem is the operational commander who wants to be his own intelligence officer.[43] Relying on his own experiences, a commander may ignore facts which actually make his experiences irrelevant. Moreover, personal bias, or unwillingness to accept legitimate differences in interpretation, poses challenges for the intelligence advisor. Perhaps it may be a fear of reliance on intelligence or simple ignorance of what intelligence offers. As was pathetically observed by Second Army Colonel Serbinovitch when excusing his own failed tactics, *"No orders for reconnaissance in this direction had been received."*[44] Startlingly, the Colonel saw no need to dispatch reconnaissance on his own. This, and other evidence, suggests that Russian commanders were disposed to minimize operational intelligence. In contrast, the Germans successfully leveraged operational intelligence to their advantage.

Hindenburg said, *"Without German aviation there would have been no Tannenberg."*[45] This may be somewhat of an exaggeration, but German pilots did provide plenty of useful intelligence. Indeed, he and Ludendorff came to rely heavily on pilot reports. The significance of air reconnaissance in 1914 resembled ULTRA in 1942.[46] The Russians had aircraft and dirigibles, but most of these assets were committed elsewhere

along the eastern front, depriving Zilinsky's Generals of this intelligence source.[47]
Nevertheless, they should have factored the German collection of this intelligence into
their own assessment of likely enemy force deployment. The Russians, knowing their
movements and force size had been observed by the enemy, should have predicted how
this information could be used against them. Better Russian troop dispersal would have
denied the Germans an easy target for aerial observation. Camouflage and concealment
would also have made observation by pilots difficult. Moreover, effective use of
deception by the Russians would have countered intelligence from both aerial
reconnaissance and espionage agent reporting.

Human sources of intelligence proved remarkably fruitful for the Germans as
did thorough prisoner interrogation and document exploitation. Clever use of agents
collecting intelligence in the Russian rear area helped immeasurably. Even the use of
Jewish refugees, presumably fleeing Russian persecution, was a source of intelligence.[48]
There is no evidence that the Russians clearly perceived the human-source intelligence
threat from peasants living in the occupied areas. As in the case of airborne observation,
use of concealment might possibly have bewildered or confused the German agents. At a
minimum, the Russians squandered the opportunity for deception and perception
management operations. Double agents, planted documents, and misleading troop
movements were not tried.[49] To make matters worse, the Russians' primary source of
battlefield intelligence, forward deployed mounted cavalry, failed miserably. This led to
miscalculations by both Rennenkampf and Samsonov. Consequently, the Russian
Generals were never aided by information gathered by troops at the forward edge of the
battlefield nor from reconnaissance on horseback.

Finally, and of utmost importance, was superb signals intelligence collection by the Germans. In addition to the fixed ground stations near Konigsberg, the Eighth Army had its own indigenous intercept gear. Intercepted messages were immediately translated and transmitted to the German Army commanders, who consequently knew the strengths, objectives, and intentions of the Russians. The magnitude of the German intercept effort was significant. They had to martial translators, code breakers, and well as radio technicians to find correct frequencies and direct antennas. Furthermore, the Germans successfully maintained adequate secrecy surrounding their signals work to prevent compromise. Conversely, Russian complete failure to understand the communications threat or to take countermeasures, magnified this German strength.[50]

Interestingly, some German accounts of the battle tend to emphasize the tactical prowess of the commanders rather than competent intelligence support. In actuality, Ludendorff came to depend on several dozen intercepts each day. Russian use of wireless in the clear continued for another year and facilitated German exploitation of this intelligence source.[51] Hoffman was more candid in acknowledging the value of the intercepts saying, *"We had an ally that I can only talk about after it is over. We knew all the enemy's plans."*[52]

Finale

Leveraging operational intelligence was the key to German victory at Tannenberg. German commanders capitalized on information superiority based on comprehensive intelligence collections of human sources, signals intercept, and imagery vis-à-vis aircraft observation. The Germans remained receptive to operational intelligence, trusting it to reduce uncertainty and change. It was incorporated into every aspect of planning, and commanders made it part of their operational art. German adaptability and intuition regarding intelligence, became force multipliers enabling them to overcome Russian superiority of numbers.

In contrast, the Russians failed to appreciate operational intelligence and the risks of ignoring their own vulnerabilities. Russian commanders made decisions with faulty or no intelligence whatsoever. Protection of their own operational intelligence seemed of no consequence - guaranteeing total destruction as an outcome.

Enduring relevance for modern military commanders is that operational intelligence can help manage uncertainty in war presuming one remains objective and flexible as the intelligence picture changes. Commanders must pay attention to the basics of operations security and not to underestimate the enemy's capabilities to collect intelligence. Indeed, operational intelligence, and the courage and flexibility to incorporate intelligence into tactical and strategic plans, can help commanders manage the enigmatics of war.

Leveraging operational intelligence will maximize surprise as a force multiplier while preventing the adversary from doing likewise, "...*giving one commander the confidence and boldness to attempt a daring maneuver, while the other commander, watching in bewilderment, allows it to succeed.*"[53] It worked for the German Eighth Army in 1914 and can work on today's technologically advanced battlefield.

END

NOTES

[1] Sun Tzu, The Art of War, trans. by Samuel B. Griffith, (New York: Oxford University Press, 1971), 129.

[2] Operational art complements strategy and tactics as components of military art. Operational art is principally concerned with aspects of planning, preparing, conducting, and sustaining major operations to accomplish operational or strategic objectives in a theater. Intelligence is the common thread that runs between all factors of operational art. An authoritative treatment of operational art, and all of its tenets, is found in Milan N. Vego, Operational Warfare, (Newport, RI: U.S. Naval War College, 2000)

[3] In chapter of seven of his influential work, Clausewitz allows for the turbulence of the physical world as causing uncertainty. *"A general in time of war is constantly bombarded by reports both true and false; by errors arising from fear or negligence or hastiness; by disobedience born of right or wrong interpretations, of ill will, or a proper or mistaken sense of duty, of laziness, or of exhaustion; and by accidents that nobody could have foreseen."* As if to counter this view of reality, he goes on to say that a commander can make sense of disorder, *"Long experience of war creates a knack of rapidly assessing these phenomena; courage and strength of character are as impervious to them as a rock to the rippling waves."* Uncertainty can be mitigated by a skilled commander. Carl von Clausewitz, On War, trans. and ed. by Sir Michael Howard and Peter Paret. (New Jersey: Princeton Press, 1976), 193.

[4] Michael I. Handel, ed. Intelligence and Military Operations, (London: Cass, 1989), 15.

[5] A discussion of how this dilemma effected the commanders of Tannenberg can be found in Dennis E. Showalter, Tannenberg, Clash of Empires, (Hamden, CT: Shoe String Press, 1991), 154 and 268.

[6] Geoffrey C. Evans, Tannenberg 1410:1914, (Pennsylvania: Stackpole Books, 1970), 65.

[7] Colonel Hoffmann was widely regarded as the best man on the German General Staff's Russian section. He had traveled extensively in that country and knew the language and the Russian military system. As a military attaché to Japan during the Russo-Japanese War, Hoffmann had been able to study the Czar's army in action from an enemy perspective. Hoffmann had the wisdom to exploit battlefield intelligence, and the skills of persuasion to convince leadership of its merit. Showalter, 142.

[8] After the war, Ludendorff wrote a book taking credit for the German victory at Tannenberg, although his accounts have been challenged. Ludendorff went on from Tannenberg to become one of the key tacticians and German military leaders of WWI. His book reflects tremendous bitterness and blame directed toward the German government. *"Germans who fought loyally for their country were delivered up by their Government to the enemy, to serve for his triumph."* Erich Ludendorff, Ludendorff's Own Story. Vol. II, (New York: Harper & Brothers, 1919), 433. In addition, he bestows liberal credit upon himself and Hindenberg for German military victories with little mention of subordinate commanders. *"But, indeed, the operations which Field-Marshal von Hindenberg and I had to conduct...rank among the most formidable in history."* Ludendorff, Vol. II, 1; See also Erich Ludendorff, Ludendorff's Own Story. Vol. I, (New York: Harper & Brothers, 1919).

[9] Richard Armstrong, "Tactical Triumph at Tannenberg," Military History, (August 1997): 58.

[10] Analysis would later show Russian wireless messages being sent in the clear, were a key advantage to the German High Command who, by interception of them, became aware of future Russian plans long before they were put into execution. Armstrong, 58; and Showalter, 169.

[11] Armstrong, 61.

[12] Showalter, 146.

[13] Reportedly, the two Russian Generals got into a fistfight after the Battle of Mukden during the Russo-Japanese War. Hostilities remained. Hoffmann shared his theory with Prittwitz and Ludendorff. As it happened, during Tannenberg, Rennenkampf never responded to Samsonov's pleas for assistance owing to fact that his own forces were weakened. In his memoirs, Hoffmann provides evidence that it was actually Rennenkampf's personal hatred which accounted for Samsonov being left on his own. Hoffmann says that *"any advance by Rennenkampf would have prevented the disaster of Tannenberg."* Max Hoffmann, War Diaries and Other Papers. Vol. I, (London: Martin Secker, 1929), 19; and Max Hoffmann, War Diaries and Other Papers. Vol. II, (London: Martin Secker, 1929), 40-41 and 314.

[14] Hoffmann, Diaries Vol. II, 25.

[15] The following is an actual message dropped into waiting German hands;
-*"Aeroplane A 29. Lieutenant Hesse. Route Eylau - Soldau - Mlawa- -Neidenburg. Time 9:15 AM."*
-*"To Commander, Ist Corps."*
-*"Column of all arms moving from Mlawa on Neidenburg. Head at Kandien, tail one kilometer N. of Mlawa. Time, 9:10 AM. A second column moving from Stupsk on Mlawa. Head at E. entrance Mlawa, tail Wola. Time 8:45 AM."*
-*"Korner, observer."*
When the war began, each Corps and 8th Army Headquarters was assigned six planes. Additionally, the intelligence stations at Konigsberg, Thron, Graudenz, and Posen had four planes each. Some crews took rifles aloft in addition to their service pistols. Sometimes, light bombs or hand grenades would be added to frighten a few horses. However, the main purpose was to gather visual intelligence. These missions were so important, that the observer, not the pilot, was in command of the two-seater aircraft. Showalter, 153 and 311; and Edmund Ironside, Tannenberg - The First Thirty Days in East Prussia, (London: William Blackwood & Sons Ltd., 1928), 190.

[16] Evans, 87.

[17] Hindenberg describes the discovery of a note in a dead Russian officer's pocket. Significant intelligence was derived from the translation and analysis of this document. Moreover, Hindenberg goes on to describe how German operational plans shifted due this one piece of intelligence. Paul von Hindenburg, Out of My Life, (London: Cassell and Company, 1920), 87.

[18] Showalter, 301.

[19] Ironside, 82.

[20] Hoffmann notes in his diaries that the preliminary framework for Tannenberg was actually the planning of Prittwitz. Hoffmann, Diaries Vol. II, 251.

[21] Ludendorff was surprised all the instructions and orders necessary for the intended attack were already given. Generally speaking, Ludendorff recognized that Prittwitz had designed an excellent plan making use of operational intelligence. Hoffmann's account attempts to resurrect Prittwitz's reputation. Hoffmann, Diaries Vol. II, 255; Furthermore, Hoffmann had effected changes in Eighth Army movement orders to reflect newly acquired intelligence. Ironside notes that Ludendorff *"...makes no mention of Hoffmann's changes in the original order to withdraw...and yet theses changes must have been made, for a study of the railway orders reveals the fact quite plainly. Ludendorff was never inclined to give credit to others where he himself might be belittled."* Ironside, 149; In later years, when Ludendorff would write his memoirs, he would disavow any such intelligence, emphasizing his own genius in defeating the Russians. Ludendorff, Ludendorff's Own Story. Vol. I, 50-55; In contrast, Hoffmann devotes an entire chapter in his memoirs to radio intercept and how operational intelligence was the key factor in the German victory. Hoffmann, Diaries Vol. II, Chapter VI, "The Wireless Messages," 265; Hindenburg also discounted signals intercept as a significant aid. Hindenberg, 84-85.

[22] Ironside, 198.

[23] Hoffmann, Diaries Vol. II, 282.

[24] In an example of unbelievably bad communications security, a Russian signal officer found a stack of telegrams in the Warsaw central telegraph office, addressed to Second Army headquarters. It was never determined how long they'd been there but yet they contained sensitive plans. Evans, 79.

[25] Ironside, 127.

[26] Showalter, 217.

[27] According to Hoffmann, "...Samsonoff [sic] issued an order to the (Second Army) to pursue. The order was sent by wireless from the Russian station, not in cipher, and we intercepted it. This was the first of countless orders that in the beginning the Russians sent, with quite incomprehensible carelessness, unciphered...This carelessness greatly facilitated the control of operations in the East, and in many cases even made the initiative possible for us". Hoffmann, Diaries Vol. II, 35.

[28] Armstrong, 64; and Showalter, 229.

[29] Ironside notes that as Second Army crumbled, the German use of signals intelligence sealed the Russians' fate, "The order giving the dispositions of the Second Army...was sent out in the clear, and it is therefore not surprising that the Germans were able to make dispositions to envelop the wretched Russian Army." See Ironside, 146; Showalter describes Hoffmann being so excited about some of the intercepts that he chased his superiors in a car and handed them a message from a moving car, "a maneuver more appropriate for a rodeo cowboy than a middle-aged staff colonel with a weight problem." Showalter, 231.

[30] Armstrong, 64; Additionally Evans' account of the last hours of Tannenberg is particularly graphic. "The constant sitting up into all hours of the night waiting for orders, the repeated alarms due to ignorance of what was happening elsewhere, and insufficient food, had taken their toll of the Russian commanders, their staffs and the troops; all were nervous, tired out and hungry. Many had no sleep for 10 nights. To add to these difficulties, the country through which the retreat had to pass was a sea of forests and lakes and, without compasses, unable to read maps with the place-names written in Roman characters, with only a few signposts to direct them, it is no wonder many lost their way during these two tragic days and particularly at night. The narrow isthmuses between the lakes and sandy tracks through the forest were crammed with unwieldy horse transport trying to escape. The rot had firmly set in and as the hours passed, bodies of men marched backwards and forwards like rabbits vainly attempting to escape from the net. Despite this, there were several instances of resolute soldiers fighting courageously until they were either killed or captured." Evans, 144

[31] Samsonov's suicide is covered in depth as well as the final chaotic hours of the Second Army. Evans, 153.

[32] Hoffmann shares his observation about the value of air reports, "...the report of an airman had come in, who said he had the impression that the principle Russian positions were only weakly occupied, or not occupied at all." Hoffmann, Diaries Vol. II, 44.

[33] In the end, Zilinsky's orders to his commanders had become increasingly reactive and uncoordinated. Furthermore, he blamed Rennenkampf for failing to control his army. Zilinsky was genuinely surprised when Grand Duke Nikolai reported to the Czar, "I am inclined to think that General Zilinsky has lost his head and in general is not capable of controlling operations." Zilinsky, not Rennenkampf, ended up being relieved of his command. Armstrong, 64.

[34] Nicholas N. Golvine, The Russian Campaign of 1914 (Fort Leavenworth, Kansas: The Command and General Staff School Press, 1933), 389.

[35] Golvine, 325.

[36] Ironside, 277.

[37] Ironside, 195; In addition, Schmitt and Vedeler assert that due to the victory at Tannenberg, Hindenberg and Ludendorff, *"gained such prestige that the general staff had to listen to the inseparable pair."* However, it was Eighth Army Operations Officer, Colonel Hoffmann who convinced his superiors how to leverage operational intelligence. *"Hindenberg and Ludendorff got the credit for the dazzling stroke, which really belonged to Hoffmann and the subordinate field commanders."* Bernadotte E. Schmitt and Harold C. Vedeler, The World in the Crucible 1914-1919 (New York: Harper & Row, 1984), 57; Hoffmann frankly observed, *"If we try to give an exact answer to the question who deserves the most credit for the victory at Tannenberg, we must also consider the conduct of the enemy, without whose blunders the success would not have been possible."* Hoffmann, Diaries Vol. II, 332.

[38] The concept of actionable intelligence is that which can be immediately utilized or which is perishable and will loose utility quickly. If an advantage or opportunity is presented by such intelligence, this fact must be brought to the commander's attention less risk being lost in the confusion of war. Conversely, a commander's plan must be flexible enough to incorporate actionable intelligence. The German victory in The Battle of Tannenberg is an example of this concept.

[39] Operational intelligence is critical to the prosecution of war. More than 2,000 years ago, Thucydides spoke of plans based on enemy intelligence, *"(while planning), it's right to rest our hopes not on a belief in (the enemy's) blunders, but on the soundness of our own provisions."* Thucydides, The History of the Peloponnesian War, trans. R. Crawley, (New York: E.P. Dutton & Co., 1950), 56; More than two centuries later, joint doctrine tells us, *"The usefulness of intelligence information...is directly proportional to its timeliness and accuracy, especially in targeting and maneuver."* Joint Chiefs of Staff, Joint Doctrine for Multinational Operations, Joint Pub 3-16 (Washington, DC: 5 April 2000), III-4.

[40] Jomini said, *"One of the surest ways of forming good combinations in war would be to order movements only after obtaining perfect information of the enemy's proceedings. In fact, how can any man say what he should do himself, if he is ignorant of what his adversary is about?"* Antoine Henri Jomini, The Art of War (Philadelphia: J.B. Lippincott, 1862), 268; and Handel, Michael I., Masters of War, 2nd ed. (London: Frank Cass & Company, 1996), 148.

[41] Jomini, 269-70.

[42] Information superiority as defined by Joint Chiefs of Staff, Joint Doctrine for Information Operations, Joint Pub 3-13 (Washington, DC: 9 October 1998), GL-7.

[43] Vego, 213.

[44] Ironside, 155.

[45] Armstrong, 80; The Germans used two different aircraft for reconnaissance. The *Aviatik B.I* was manufactured by Automobil und Aviatikwerke. Weighing 2,400 lbs, it's top speed was 62mph. The *Taube* was made by Albatros Werke among others. Weighing 2,257 lbs, it could fly 60 mph. Both planes carried two persons and had a 4 hour flight duration. Ira Boucher, "German Aviation 1914," An Illustrated History of WWI, http://www.wwiavaition.com/german1914.shtml [25 April 2001].

[46] ULTRA was a WWII source codeword for intercepted German communications after the Allies broke the German encryption. Like ULTRA, air reconnaissance intelligence generated skepticism while at the same time, was credited with magical accuracy. Showalter, 312.

[47] There were only a few Russian aircraft sorties. One mission in particular highlighted the sometimes confusing nature of this newly-employed intelligence resource. At the direction of Russian General Kluyev of XIII Corps, one airplane was dispatched to check positions of other Russian units. The observer reported a corps-strength force marching westward though he'd been unable to determine if the troops were German or Russian. XIII Corps staff was convinced the airman had spotted a Russian unit advancing as ordered. Kluyev promptly sent the pilot back with a message for the Russian commander with orders to land beside the column

and see the dispatch was received. Flying low as ordered, the plane was brought down by a fusillade of rifle fire. Both the pilot and his captors were surprised at his arrival. The column was advancing Germans, not Russians. Showalter, 267.

[48] Hoffmann, <u>War Diaries. Vol. II</u>, 24.

[49] Offensive counterintelligence measures to foil German intelligence efforts were ineffective or non-existent. There is no evidence that the Russians attempted to exploit German human sources with perception management or recruitment as double agents. Neither is there evidence of planting false information for German collection. Any appreciation for German signals collection, would have suggested transmitting false orders to confuse radio monitors. There is no evidence the Russians tried this either.

[50] According to one analysis, *"Since their intelligence functions were almost nonexistent, the Russians developed no useful intelligence about the enemy's intentions, distribution of forces, or movements; the Germans, on the other hand, intercepted Russian radio messages sent in the clear or in easily decipherable code, revealing the schedule of movement of the Russian armies, the objectives of individual corps, the strength of forces."* Schmitt, 57.

[51] Philip Neame, <u>German Strategy in the Great War</u> (London: Edward Arnold & Company, 1923), 52.

[52] Hoffmann's accounts are surprisingly candid and unpretentious. He shares credit with all the key German Generals and makes the observation that there was no one particular commander who won Tannenberg. As an intelligence practitioner, Hoffmann gives tremendous weight to the value of operational intelligence. Many scholars of Tannenberg credit Hoffmann with being a strong advocate of intelligence, to the benefit to his superiors. Hoffmann, <u>War Diaries. Vol. I</u>, 41.

[53] Armstrong, 80.

Bibliography

Armstrong, Richard N. "Tactical Triumph at Tannenberg." Military History, (Aug 1997): 58-64+.

Boucher, Ira. "German Aviation 1914." An Illustrated History of WWI.
  http://www.wwiavaition.com/german1914.shtml [25 April 2001].

von Clausewitz, Carl. On War. Translated and edited by Sir Michael Howard and Peter Paret.
  New Jersey: Princeton Press, 1976.

Evans, Geoffery C. Tannenberg 1410 : 1914, Pennsylvania: Stackpole Books, 1970.

Golvine, Nicholas N. The Russian Campaign of 1914, Fort Leavenworth, Kansas: The
  Command and General Staff School Press, 1933.

Handel, Michael I. Masters of War, 2nd ed. London: Frank Cass & Company, 1996.

Handel, Michael I., ed. Intelligence and Military Operations, London: Frank Cass &
  Company, 1990.

von Hoffmann, Max. War Diaries and Other Papers. Vol. I, London: Martin Secker, 1929.

von Hoffmann, Max. War Diaries and Other Papers. Vol. II, London: Martin Secker, 1929.

von Hindenburg, Paul. Out of My Life, London: Cassell and Company, 1920.

Ironside, Edmund. Tannenberg - The First Thirty Days in East Prussia, London: William
  Blackwood & Sons Ltd., 1928.

Jomini, Baron Antoine Henri. The Art of War, Philadelphia: J.B. Lippincott, 1862.

von Ludendorff, Erich. Ludendorff's Own Story. Vol. I, New York: Harper & Brothers,
  1919.

von Ludendorff, Erich. Ludendorff's Own Story. Vol. II, New York: Harper & Brothers,
  1919.

Neame, Philip. German Strategy in the Great War, London: Edward Arnold & Company,
  1923.

Schmitt, Bernadotte E. and Harold C. Vedeler. The World in the Crucible 1914-1919, New
  York: Harper & Row, 1984.

Showalter, Dennis E. Tannenberg, Clash of Empires, Hamden, CT: Shoe String Press, 1991.

Sun Tzu, <u>The Art of War</u>. Translated by Samuel B. Griffith. New York: Oxford University
    Press, 1971.

Thucydides, <u>The History of the Peloponnesian War</u>. Translated by R. Crawley. New York:
    E.P. Dutton & Co., 1950.

U.S. Joint Chiefs of Staff, <u>Doctrine for Intelligence Support to Joint Operations</u>, Joint Pub 2-
    0. Washington, DC: 9 March 2000.

U.S. Joint Chiefs of Staff, <u>Joint Doctrine for Information Operations</u>, Joint Pub 3-13.
    Washington, DC: 9 October 1998.

U.S. Joint Chiefs of Staff, <u>Joint Doctrine for Multinational Operations</u>, Joint Pub 3-16.
    Washington, DC: 5 April 2000.

Vego, Milan N. <u>Operational Warfare</u>, Newport, RI: U.S. Naval War College, 2000.

www.ingramcontent.com/pod-product-compliance
Lightning Source LLC
Chambersburg PA
CBHW080759290526
45790CB00008B/3509